S0-BRX-040

EXPLORING OUR SOLAR SYSTEM

MIGHTY MEGAPLANETS

JUPITER AND SATURN

DAVID JEFFERIS

Crabtree Publishing Company

www.crabtreebooks.com

■ THE MEGAPLANETS

The "megaplanets" of the **solar system** are Jupiter and Saturn. These are the biggest planets, and they are much larger than our own planet, Earth. Jupiter and Saturn may belong to the same solar system as Earth, but they have little else in common with Earth. Earth is a **rocky planet**, with a solid surface, or **crust**. Jupiter and Saturn are made mostly of gases, and have no solid surface at all. Jupiter and Saturn do have many rocky **moons**, ranging in size from a few miles across to big enough to have an **atmosphere**.

Crabtree Publishing Company

PMB 16A,
350 Fifth Avenue, Suite 3308
New York, NY 10118

616 Welland Avenue,
St. Catharines, Ontario
L2M 5V6

Published by Crabtree
Publishing Company
© 2009

Written and produced by:
    David Jefferis/Buzz Books
Educational advisor:
    Julie Stapleton
Science advisor:
    Mat Irvine FBIS
Editor: Ellen Rodger
Copy editor:
    Adrianna Morganelli
Proofreader: Crystal Sikkens
Project editor: Robert Walker
Production coordinator:
    Katherine Kantor

■ ACKNOWLEDGEMENTS

We wish to thank all those people who have helped to create this publication. Information and images were supplied by:

Agencies and organizations:
    Ciclops Cassini Central
        Imaging Laboratory
    CIT California Institute of Technology
    ESA European Space Agency
    IAU International Astronomical Union
    JPL Jet Propulsion Laboratory
    NASA National Aeronautics and
        Space Administration

Collections and individuals:
    Alpha Archive
    Donald E. Davis
    David Jefferis
    Bjorn Johnsson

Library and Archives Canada Cataloguing in Publication

Jefferis, David
    Mighty megaplanets : Jupiter and Saturn / David Jefferis.

(Exploring our solar system)
Includes index.
ISBN 978-0-7787-3737-7 (bound).--ISBN 978-0-7787-3753-7 (pbk.)

    1. Jupiter (Planet)--Juvenile literature. 2. Saturn (Planet)--Juvenile literature. I. Title. II. Series: Exploring our solar system (St. Catharines, Ont.)

QB661.J43 2008   j523.45   C2008-903110-5

Library of Congress Cataloging-in-Publication Data

Jefferis, David.
    Mighty megaplanets : Jupiter and Saturn / David Jefferis.
        p. cm. -- (Exploring our solar system)
    Includes index.
    ISBN-13: 978-0-7787-3753-7 (pbk. : alk. paper)
    ISBN-10: 0-7787-3753-5 (pbk. : alk. paper)
    ISBN-13: 978-0-7787-3737-7 (reinforced library binding : alk. paper)
    ISBN-10: 0-7787-3737-3 (reinforced library binding : alk. paper)
    1. Jupiter (Planet)--Juvenile literature. 2. Saturn (Planet)--Juvenile literature. I. Title. II. Series.

    QB661.J44 2009
    523.45--dc22

                                        2008021202

CONTENTS

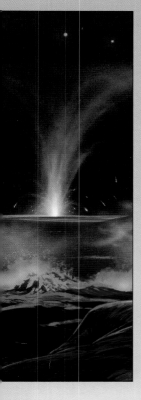

■ WHAT ARE MEGAPLANETS?

They are the biggest planets in the solar system. Jupiter alone is more massive than all the other planets put together.

■ HOW BIG ARE THEY?

Jupiter is a giant planet, 88,736 miles (142,800 km) across. Saturn is also huge when compared to Earth, but it is smaller than Jupiter, at 74,130 miles or (119,300 km) across.

Jupiter

■ **Jupiter and Saturn are shown here to scale with a much smaller Earth.**

Earth is 7,927 miles (12,756 km) across

Saturn

■ WHAT DO THEIR NAMES MEAN?

As the biggest planet, Jupiter was named by the ancient Romans after their "king of the gods." Saturn is also a Roman name, after Saturnus, the Roman god of farming and the harvest.

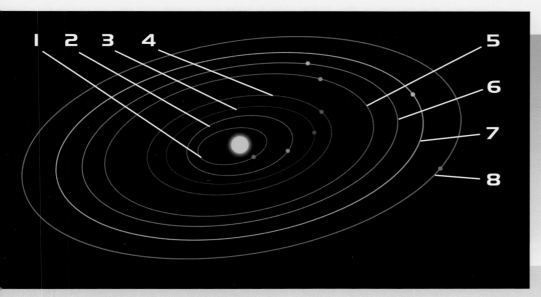

Like the other planets of the solar system, Jupiter and Saturn follow a long, curving path around the sun, called an orbit.

1	Mercury	5	Jupiter
2	Venus	6	Saturn
3	Earth	7	Uranus
4	Mars	8	Neptune

WOW!
Their distance from the sun makes the megaplanets' orbits very large. Jupiter takes 11.9 Earth-years to complete one orbit. Saturn takes 29.5 years.

HOW FAR AWAY FROM THE SUN ARE THEY?

Both megaplanets are further from the sun than Earth. Jupiter orbits at an average distance of 485 million miles (780 million km), compared with Earth's 93 million miles (108 million km). Saturn is even further away, at 890 million miles (1433 million km). The distances vary a little, because planets do not orbit the sun in exact circles.

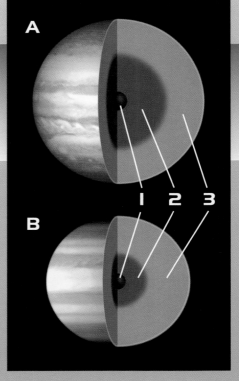

In the center of Jupiter (A) and Saturn (B) there may be a small rocky core (1). Around this is a sphere of metallic hydrogen (2), or hydrogen gas that has been crushed to form a kind of super-hard, super-dense solid metal. Liquid hydrogen (3) lies above this, before the upper atmosphere.

WHAT ARE JUPITER AND SATURN MADE OF?

Jupiter and Saturn are also called "gas giants," because they are big balls of gases, rather than rocky planets like Earth. If you flew to either planet, you could not land on them. Instead of a solid surface, the clouds would get thicker and thicker, until the pressure was high enough to crush your spacecraft to a pulp – which was the fate of a space probe launched into Jupiter's clouds in 1995.

■WHEN WERE THE MEGAPLANETS FORMED?

Jupiter and Saturn are thought to have formed at the same time as the other planets and the sun, about 4.6 billion years ago.

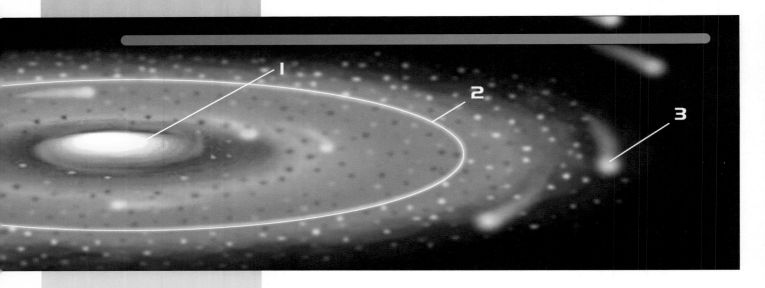

■ Temperatures beyond the newly-forming sun (1) fell rapidly with distance from it. Beyond the frost line (2) water-ice stayed as a solid, making a good building block for the megaplanets (3).

■ HOW DID JUPITER AND SATURN FORM?

Scientists think that the solar system – the sun, the planets, and other space material – formed from a huge, slowly turning frisbee-shaped cloud of gas, dust, and rocks. Jupiter and Saturn formed in the outer regions of this cloud. Planets such as Earth formed much closer to the sun.

■ HOW DID PLANET FORMATION TAKE PLACE?

It is thought that over time, in a process called **accretion**, billions of tiny dust particles in the gas cloud collided and stuck together to form bigger ones. These slowly grew enough to be the size of mini-planets, called planetesimals. These planetesimals then attracted most of the remaining material, to finally become the planets we know today.

WOW!
There are many bits and pieces left over from the formation of the solar system. Today, billions of chunks of ice and rock still drift in space between the planets.

Young sun starts to glow

Huge disk, made of dust, ice, and rocks

Computer simulation shows planets forming

■ WHY DID THE MEGAPLANETS BECOME SO BIG?

This is because of the frost line, the point in space at which water stays frozen as ice rather than becoming a gas. Ice formed a good "glue" between particles, and so the megaplanets could grow more easily than planets such as Earth. They grew so big that they were able to attract gases such as hydrogen and **helium**, to become gas giants.

■ In the early days of its formation, the solar system could have looked much like the big picture above.

In the center of the disk is the young sun, recently "turned on," when it became hot enough to start glowing.

Surrounding the sun is the material that will form the planets.

HOW DO WE KNOW ABOUT THE MEGAPLANETS?

Most of our information comes from studies made by space probes, which have flown on missions since the 1970s.

WHAT WERE PIONEER 10 AND 11?

These were the first space probes to fly near Jupiter, in 1973 and 1974. They briefly studied Jupiter's **magnetic field** and atmosphere. They also took pictures of the cloud belts.

Galileo's Jupiter oven-sized atmosphere probe sent signals for just over an hour, until the gas pressure around it reached 338 lb/sq in (23 bar). Then the probe's casing failed, and the instruments inside were crushed.

AND THE VOYAGERS?

These were two more probes that flew past Jupiter in March and July 1979, on their way to the outer solar system. The Voyager probes took the first detailed pictures of Jupiter's moons, and noted powerful lightning flashes deep in the atmosphere.

WHAT WAS GALILEO'S JUPITER MISSION?

Galileo was a space probe that spent several years studying Jupiter and its moons. In 1995, a Galileo 'first' was to send a probe into the atmosphere to find out what was under the cloud-tops. Galileo studied Jupiter and its moons for eight years in all, before running low on fuel in 2003.

WOW!
Galileo made some very close fly-bys of Jupiter's moons. The nearest of these was to swoop past the volcanic moon Io, at a distance of under 200 miles (320 km).

◼ WHAT ABOUT MISSIONS TO SATURN?

One of the Pioneers and both Voyagers flew past Saturn. But the most important Saturn probe is called Cassini-Huygens, which has studied the megaplanet and its moons since 2004.

◼ Galileo passes Amalthea, a potato-shaped moon of Jupiter. Amalthea is about 155 miles (250 km) on its longest side.

◼ The 22-foot long (6.8m) Cassini space probe has studied Saturn, its huge rings, and many moons since arriving there in July 2004.

Cassini also carried a separate mini-probe, called the Huygens lander. In 2005, Cassini launched Huygens toward Saturn's big moon Titan, on which it landed safely.

■ DOES JUPITER HAVE RINGS?

Yes it does, but they are nothing like Saturn's amazing rings. Instead, they are almost invisible, being made up of tiny dust particles.

■ The rings consist of two very thin rings (1,2), the main ring (3), and the halo ring (4).

Orbiting in the rings are four moons: Amalthea (5), Adrastea (6), Metis (7) and Thebe (8).

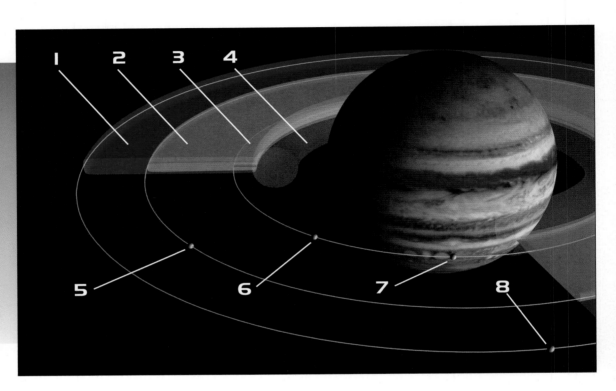

■ WHAT ARE JUPITER'S RINGS MADE OF?

They are made mostly of incredibly tiny dust particles. These are about 100 times smaller than the width of a human hair, so it is not surprising that the rings were only discovered in 1979, when the Voyager 1 space probe flew past Jupiter. At their widest, the rings spread across 140,000 miles (225,000 km), but because they are so fine, they contain only as much matter as one of Jupiter's smaller moons.

WOW!
Jupiter spins so fast – once almost every 10 hours – that it is not a perfect sphere. Instead, it bulges around the equator to look slightly squashed.

■ WHERE DOES THE DUST COME FROM?

The rings are made of material from the four nearby moons, thrown off by explosions caused by the impacts of **meteors** (rocks drifting through space). The moons are small, with very low **gravity**, so most debris flies off into space, rather than falling back to the surface.

Earth also has a magnetic field

■ Jupiter's magnetic field (blue lines) helps create the Io "flux tube." This is a magnetic region between Io (arrowed) and Jupiter, shaped like a thin donut.

□ Magnetism also traps particles from the sun, to create glowing auroras around the poles.

■ IS JUPITER MAGNETIC?

Yes – its magnetic field is thousands of times stronger than that of Earth and Saturn. Jupiter's field is created in the huge sphere of metallic hydrogen around its core, where swirling movements create powerful electric currents. These generate the huge magnetic field.

HOW BIG IS THE GREAT RED SPOT?

The Great Red Spot is the biggest single feature on Jupiter and it is HUGE! Our own planet, Earth, could be swallowed completely by the Great Red Spot.

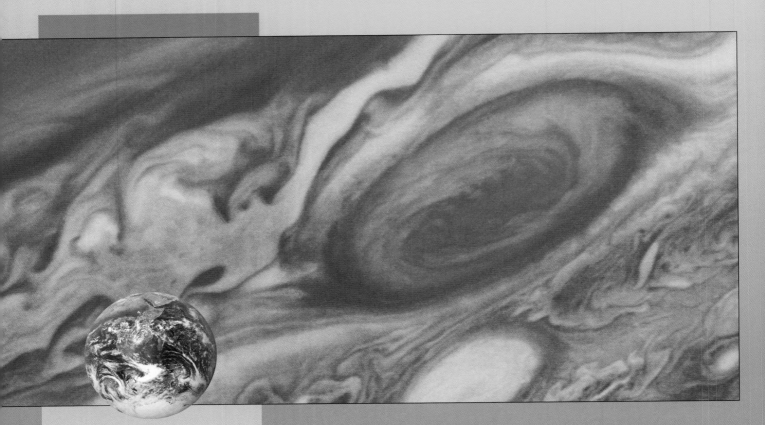

■ Here Earth is shown to scale with the Great Red Spot. Gases blasting around the edges of the Spot roar along at speeds of nearly 300 mph (483 km/h).

■ WHAT EXACTLY IS THE GREAT RED SPOT?

It is a huge storm that swirls in the atmosphere of Jupiter. It is most likely a planet-sized **eddy**, caused by warm gases rising from below, mixing with colder gases higher up.

■ HOW LONG HAS IT BEEN RAGING?

The Great Red Spot was probably first seen in 1665, by the Italian astronomer Giovanni Cassini. It may have been there for hundreds of years.

WOW!
Jupiter also has white and brown storms. White ones are made of cool clouds. Brown are warmer. They can last for a few hours or for many years.

□ **Red Jr. (arrowed) formed when three small spots joined together in 2000. It has turned from white to red, probably because of sulphur gases sucked up from below.**

■ HAS THE SPOT CHANGED SIZE?

Yes, it is getting smaller. Although the Great Red Spot is still huge, at 25,000 miles (40,000 km) across, it has shrunk in size by half since the early 1900s. At this rate, the Spot could be gone completely by 2050. Or it may start growing again—nobody knows for sure! There is also another, smaller storm nearby, called Red Jr. or Oval BA. The two storms have passed each other several times, and they may merge together at some point in the future.

■ WHAT WAS THE COMET CRASH?

In 1994, a **comet** – a giant 'snowball' made of ice, rocks and dust – collided with Jupiter. The comet was called Shoemaker-Levy, after the astronomers who discovered it. Before it hit Jupiter, Shoemaker-Levy broke up into pieces, and struck the megaplanet in a series of huge explosions. Closeup pictures were taken by the Galileo space probe that was near Jupiter at the time.

■ **Shoemaker-Levy hurtled toward Jupiter at nearly 40 miles/second (64 km/sec). The pieces burned up in huge fireballs when they hit the planet's atmosphere. If they had hit Earth, entire countries could have been destroyed.**

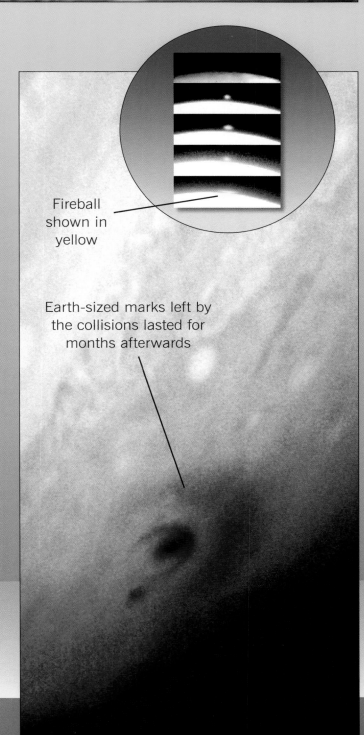

Fireball shown in yellow

Earth-sized marks left by the collisions lasted for months afterwards

◼ WHAT LIES UNDER JUPITER'S CLOUD-TOPS?

Under the visible "surface" of Jupiter are a series of cloud layers made of different mixtures of gases.

◼ WHAT GASES ARE THE CLOUDS MADE OF?

Jupiter's upper atmosphere is about 90 percent hydrogen and 10 percent helium, plus small amounts of other gases and chemicals. High white clouds are made of crystals of frozen ammonia. Further down, clouds are colored by traces of chemicals, such as sulphur and phosphorus.

◼ **The Great Red Spot is not just a feature of Jupiter's cloud-tops. It forms deep inside the atmosphere.**

Swirling hurricane cone

◼ **This view looks up at Jupiter from directly under its South Pole.**

   The atmosphere has many bands of cloud. The light-colored ones are called zones, the darker ones are called belts. The Great Red Spot (circled) drifts from east to west, but does not move north or south.

◼ COULD I BREATHE THE AIR?

No – there is little or no oxygen in Jupiter's atmosphere, and oxygen is a vital gas that most life on Earth needs to survive.

■ Jupiter and Saturn are made largely of gases, which makes them less dense than small, rocky worlds such as Earth.

Jupiter is big enough to contain 1,300 planets the size of Earth. Its mass – the amount of matter it contains – is just 318 times as great.

This means that its density is only a little more than water. If you could fill a huge bathtub, Jupiter would slowly sink in the water. Saturn is even less dense – it would float!

■ HOW HOT IS JUPITER?

Jupiter is a long way from the sun, and its outer cloud layers are very cold, at about -230°F (-145°C). The planet is warmer than the heat it gets from the sun alone. This could be because the core is still hot from its formation billions of years ago. Also, the planet is slowly shrinking, and this may be creating heat, too.

■HOW BIG ARE JUPITER'S MOONS?

Many of Jupiter's 60-plus moons are tiny, but some of them are the size of small planets.

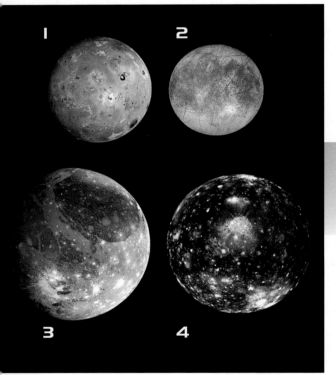

■ WHAT ARE THE GALILEAN MOONS?

These are the four biggest moons of Jupiter. They are named after the Italian astronomer Galileo Galilei, who first spotted them in 1610. Galileo used a small telescope which he had made himself.

■ **The Galilean moons are Io (1), Europa (2), Ganymede (3), and Callisto (4). The biggest of the four is Ganymede, which is 3,270 miles (5,262 km) across, a little bigger than the planet Mercury.**

■ WHAT ABOUT THE OTHER MOONS?

Most are less than seven miles (11 km) across, and some are just large chunks of rock. We know that Jupiter has at least 63 moons, but there are probably many more smaller ones waiting to be found.

■ **Europa is a target for future space missions, because it is thought to have water under the icy surface – and some scientists think life could exist there.**
Europa is thought to have an iron-nickel core (1), surrounded by rock (2). Under the frozen surface (3) lies water. However, Europa might be too cold for the water to stay liquid. Instead, there may be an ocean of slushy ice (4).

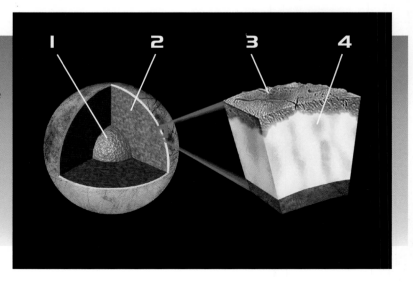

Huge plume of gas from a volcano

Jupiter

■ WHY IS THE MOON IO A BRIGHT ORANGE COLOR?

Io (pronounced *eye-oh*) is a spectacular moon, with up to 400 erupting **volcanoes**, making it the most explosive place in the solar system. Much of Io is brightly colored in shades of yellow-orange, because the volcanoes spew out a lot of sulphur, which is a yellowish substance. Many of Io's volcanoes are super powerful and some plumes of gas and dust blow more than 300 miles (483 km) into space!

■ If you could go on a space mission to Io, this is the sort of view you might see out of your spacecraft. Nearby are bubbling volcanic pits, while near the horizon an eruption blasts gas and dust high above the ground. Hanging in the sky behind is Jupiter. At this distance its bands of cloud are easy to see.

■ WHAT ARE SATURN'S RINGS MADE OF?

The vast and beautiful ring system is made almost entirely of ice particles. They range in size from tiny grains to large boulders.

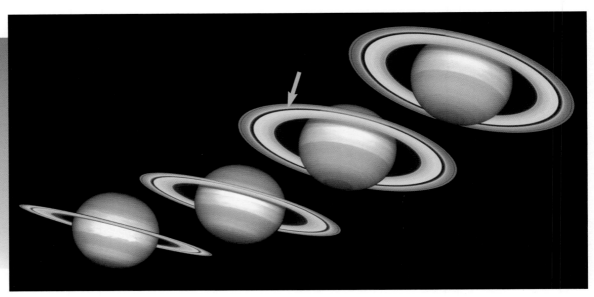

■ Our view of the rings changes as Saturn moves in its orbit around the sun. When the rings are edge-on, they can hardly be seen at all.

■ HOW MANY RINGS ARE THERE?

From a distance it looks as if Saturn has just a few, solid rings. However, the rings are really one huge, flat disk of particles, each particle moving in its own orbit around Saturn. The ringed look is because particles of various sizes cluster together, and reflect sunlight differently — some brighter, some darker.

Even gaps in the rings, such the Cassini Division (arrowed above), are not empty. They are mostly filled with fewer or smaller particles that do not reflect sunlight well, so the gaps seem dimmer or even transparent.

WOW!
The wispy F-ring is something of a puzzle, as it is not really a ring at all. Instead, the F-ring seems to be a spiral-shape that winds at least three times around Saturn.

■ HOW DID THE RINGS FORM?

We are not sure, but it is likely they are the remains of a shattered moon of Saturn, about 200 miles (300 km) across. The rings could date back to the early days of the solar system, about four billion years ago.

■ This picture shows how a ring might look if you were close to it. Groups of icy particles (these are the size of large boulders) join together to form the seemingly solid parts of the rings. They are not solid at all — the clumps constantly shift to and fro, as they are pushed and pulled by gravity from Saturn and its moons.

A   B   C   D   F   G   E

■ This view of Saturn's rings (labelled A-G above) was taken by the Cassini space probe in 2007. The picture was enhanced to show the faint G- and E-rings. Despite being so wide, the rings are very thin — even the bright B-ring is only a few feet thick!

■ **WHO FIRST SAW THE RINGS?**

They were another discovery of Galileo Galilei, who first saw them in 1610. Galileo could not make out exactly what they were through his small telescope. It was only in 1655 that a Dutch astronomer, Christiaan Huygens, realized the truth: that they were giant rings.

■ Fine details in the rings are shown in this specially-colored picture, taken by the Cassini space probe.

HOW MANY MOONS ORBIT AROUND SATURN?

Saturn comes a close second to Jupiter, with 60 named moons. If you add up even a few of the smaller moonlets, there are probably hundreds!

■ **The rocky moon Phoebe is only about 137 miles (220 km) across. Like most of the smaller moons, it is boulder-shaped, and not a sphere.**

■ WHY SO MANY MOONS?

There is no complete answer to this, but it is likely that Saturn's small moons, and even smaller moonlets, are made of material left over from the cosmic crash that made the ring system. Several small moons even orbit Saturn within the rings.

■ WHY ARE ONLY SEVEN OF SATURN'S MOONS ROUND?

It's because they are the only ones big enough to be in hydrostatic equilibrium. This simply means that there is enough matter (or mass) in a space object for its own gravity to collapse it into a sphere shape. Gravity is the force of attraction between all objects, and its strength depends on distance and mass. Stars, planets, and bigger moons all have enough mass to do this. Most of Saturn's moons are just not big enough.

WOW!
Saturn's moon Mimas is nicknamed the Death Star. This is because it has a massive crater, making it look like the huge war machine from the *Star Wars* movies.

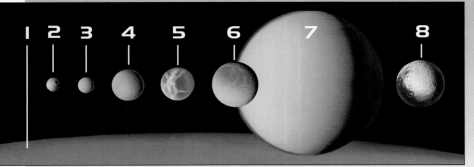

■ **Here is a lineup of the biggest moons of Saturn, shown to scale with the edge of the giant planet itself.**

1 Saturn	5 Dione
2 Mimas	6 Rhea
3 Enceladus	7 Titan
4 Tethys	8 Iapetus

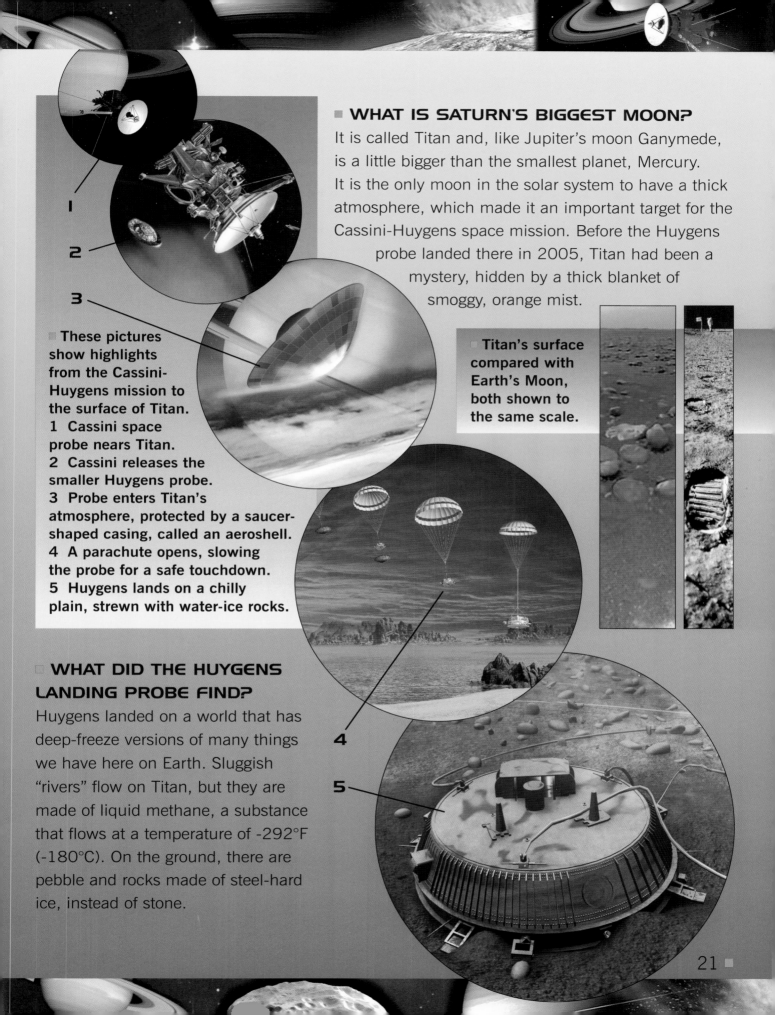

■ WHAT IS SATURN'S BIGGEST MOON?

It is called Titan and, like Jupiter's moon Ganymede, is a little bigger than the smallest planet, Mercury. It is the only moon in the solar system to have a thick atmosphere, which made it an important target for the Cassini-Huygens space mission. Before the Huygens probe landed there in 2005, Titan had been a mystery, hidden by a thick blanket of smoggy, orange mist.

■ These pictures show highlights from the Cassini-Huygens mission to the surface of Titan.
1 Cassini space probe nears Titan.
2 Cassini releases the smaller Huygens probe.
3 Probe enters Titan's atmosphere, protected by a saucer-shaped casing, called an aeroshell.
4 A parachute opens, slowing the probe for a safe touchdown.
5 Huygens lands on a chilly plain, strewn with water-ice rocks.

■ Titan's surface compared with Earth's Moon, both shown to the same scale.

■ WHAT DID THE HUYGENS LANDING PROBE FIND?

Huygens landed on a world that has deep-freeze versions of many things we have here on Earth. Sluggish "rivers" flow on Titan, but they are made of liquid methane, a substance that flows at a temperature of -292°F (-180°C). On the ground, there are pebble and rocks made of steel-hard ice, instead of stone.

21

■WHAT ARE SHEPHERD MOONS?

These are moons that orbit Saturn within the ring system. They stir up patterns and other movements in the ring particles.

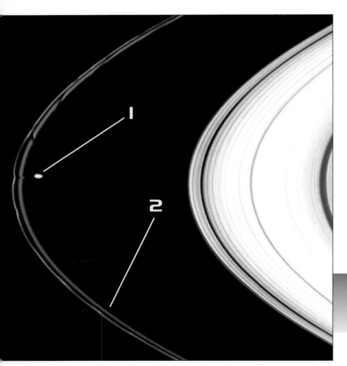

■ WHAT IS PROMETHEUS?

Prometheus (1) is one of two small moons that orbit Saturn next to the F-ring (2). Prometheus is less than 100 miles (161 km) long, and you would weigh only a few ounces on it. Even this low gravity is enough to affect the nearby F-ring, by keeping ring particles at the edges together and sucking away stragglers. Because Prometheus, and its twin moon Pandora, tend to keep the F-ring in place, they are called shepherd moons.

◻ **Particles in the F-ring swirl in kinks and knots as Prometheus passes by in its nearby orbit.**

■ WHY DO STRANGE SPOKE PATTERNS SOMETIMES APPEAR IN THE RINGS?

Spokes were first spotted by the Voyager 1 space probe in 1970, but they come and go over time. There were none to be seen when the Cassini probe neared Saturn in 2004. The spokes are made of tiny dust particles, about 50 times thinner than a human hair. It is thought they appear when magnetized by changing conditions in the rings, as Saturn orbits the sun. Then they leap up just above the surface of the ring for a while.

WOW!
Despite its size, Saturn's gravity is a little less than Earth's. Something weighing 100 lb (45.4 kg) on Earth would be about 93 lb (42 kg) on Saturn.

◻ **Spoke-like marks (arrowed) in the rings of Saturn, as seen by Voyager 1.**

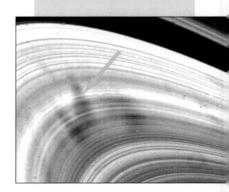

■ WHAT DOES SATURN LOOK LIKE FROM ITS MOONS?

Future space explorers, and one day, perhaps even some space tourists, may enjoy finding out, because the spectacular view will be different from every one of the many moons.

From the closer moons, Saturn's pale bands of cloud will be easy to see. The planet's rapid 10.6-hour rotation means that you should be able to see it turning slowly as you watch!

■ The pictures above show the views you might see from two of Saturn's moons. From the outer moon Iapetus (top), Saturn looks like a beautiful Christmas ornament.
From the closer moon Enceladus (above), Saturn hangs huge just above the horizon. Nearby, a geyser spurts water vapor from jagged cracks in the surface of the chilly moonscape.

■ HOW FAST DO WINDS BLOW ON SATURN?

They can blow with blinding speed – the atmosphere has super-speed winds that howl along at more than 1,100 mph (1,800 km/h)!

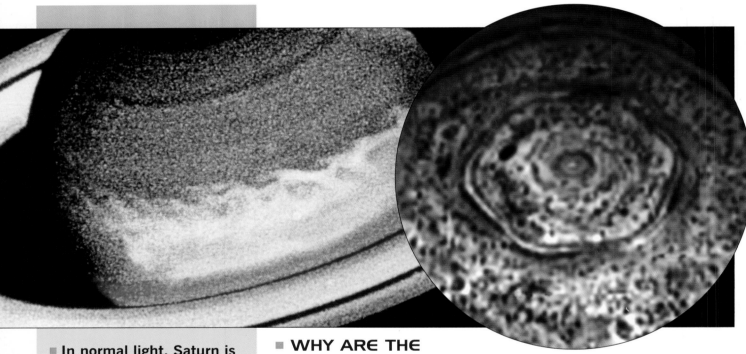

■ In normal light, Saturn is a pale creamy color. Here, color filters show details of the cloud bands that circle the planet. At the North Pole is a cloud feature called the **polar** hexagon. **Why it is this weird, six-sided shape, is not yet known for certain.**

■ WHY ARE THE WINDS SO FAST?

The fast winds are a result of Saturn's rotation speed. Despite Saturn's huge size, a day is under 11 hours long! Like Jupiter, bands of cloud circle the planet, with white spots and ovals that come and go. These are thought to be storms.

■ Like Jupiter and Earth, Saturn has bright auroras surrounding its polar regions.

■ WHAT ARE THE CLOUDS MADE OF?

They vary with height. Lower layers contain water-ice, while higher up there are ammonia clouds, with hydrogen layers above that. Saturn's atmosphere is very cold. At middle heights, the ammonia-ice particles are -243°F (-153°C).

This is the scene you might see if you could fly through the upper atmosphere of Saturn. Here, the sun is just rising, as dawn breaks across this huge planet.

In the sky above soars a mighty arch, glowing in the light of the distant sun. This is your grandstand view of the incredible ring system that surrounds Saturn.

■ COULD I BREATHE SATURN'S ATMOSPHERE?

No. A single lungful would kill you. For starters, the atmosphere is intensely cold, so your lungs would freeze solid in an instant. And much of the upper atmosphere contains ammonia, which is a deadly poison.

■ WHAT ARE THE GREAT WHITE SPOTS?

These are storms, similar to Jupiter's Great Red Spot. They appear about every 30 years.

■ HOW CAN I OBSERVE THE MEGAPLANETS?

Jupiter and Saturn are both easy-to-spot nighttime space objects. A good pair of binoculars or a small telescope will reveal the Galilean moons.

Galilean moons can be seen as points of light

■ WHAT EQUIPMENT DO I NEED?

Jupiter and Saturn are too far away to see much detail, except with a very powerful professional telescope. It is really interesting to go out on a dark night and view the sky. A pair of binoculars is all you need for planet-spotting, but it is important that they are suitable.

WOW!
In the 29.5 years it takes Saturn to orbit the sun, our view of the rings changes slowly, from edge-on, to the amazing view when they show an open angle to us.

■ WHAT KIND OF BINOCULARS ARE THE BEST TO USE?

For best results, you need a pair of binoculars labelled 7x50 or 8x50. The first number is how much they magnify the image, but the second number is more important. This is the diameter of the lens in millimeters: the bigger it is, the more light each lens gathers. A pair of 7x50 binoculars will show you Jupiter's Galilean moons (top picture) as tiny, glowing pinpricks in the sky.

■ **A pair of 7x50 binoculars can show a bright image at night. Planet-watching can be chilly work, so you might want to bring along a pair of warm gloves.**

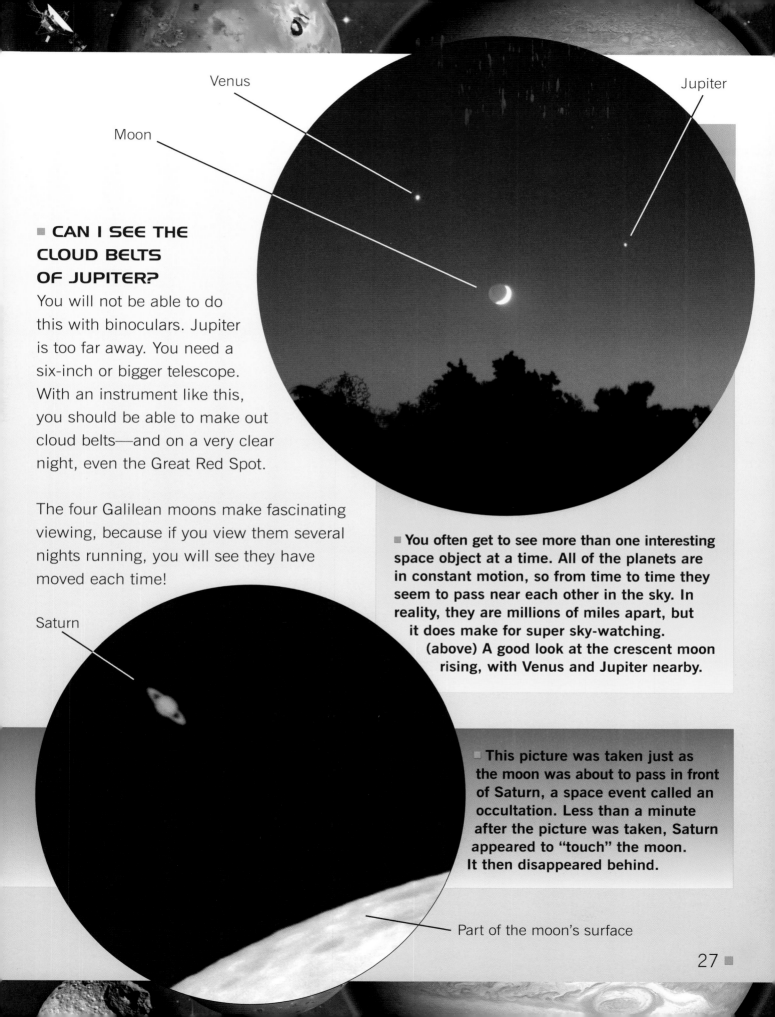

Venus

Jupiter

Moon

▪ CAN I SEE THE CLOUD BELTS OF JUPITER?

You will not be able to do this with binoculars. Jupiter is too far away. You need a six-inch or bigger telescope. With an instrument like this, you should be able to make out cloud belts—and on a very clear night, even the Great Red Spot.

The four Galilean moons make fascinating viewing, because if you view them several nights running, you will see they have moved each time!

Saturn

▪ You often get to see more than one interesting space object at a time. All of the planets are in constant motion, so from time to time they seem to pass near each other in the sky. In reality, they are millions of miles apart, but it does make for super sky-watching.
(above) A good look at the crescent moon rising, with Venus and Jupiter nearby.

▪ This picture was taken just as the moon was about to pass in front of Saturn, a space event called an occultation. Less than a minute after the picture was taken, Saturn appeared to "touch" the moon. It then disappeared behind.

Part of the moon's surface

27 ▪

■ FACTS AND FIGURES

■ JUPITER STATISTICS

Diameter

88,736 miles (142,800 km), making Jupiter the biggest planet in the solar system.

Time to rotate (day)

Jupiter turns once every 9 hours 50 minutes. It is the fastest-spinning planet.

Time to orbit once around the sun (year)

Jupiter completes one orbit of the sun every 11.7 Earth-years.

Distance to the sun

Roughly 485 million miles (780 million km).

Composition

Jupiter is thought to have a rocky core, perhaps several times the size of Earth. This is surrounded by layers of metallic hydrogen and liquid hydrogen.

Temperature

Across the planet, temperatures average about -186°F (-121°C). The cloud-tops are colder than layers deep within the atmosphere.

Surface gravity

Here on Earth we live under a force of one gravity, or 1G. Jupiter has a gravity pull of about 2.4G.

Atmosphere

Jupiter's atmosphere is about 90 percent hydrogen, 10 percent helium. Ammonia, methane, and sulphur are present in smaller amounts.

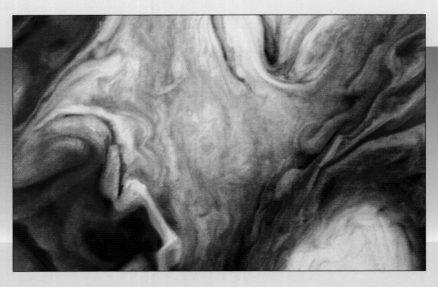

■ The different shades in the clouds of Jupiter are caused by chemicals rising to the top of the clouds from far below.
  Lightning flashes in the deeper cloud layers have been measured at more than 1,000 times stronger than any lightning seen on Earth.

■ SATURN STATISTICS

Diameter

At 74,130 miles (119,300 km) across, Saturn is the solar system's second largest planet. Its fast spin means the equator bulges outward, making the planet about 8,000 miles (13,000 km) wider than from north to south.

Time to rotate (day)

Saturn turns once about every 10 hours 36 minutes.

Time to orbit once around the sun (year)

Saturn completes one orbit of the sun every 29.5 Earth-years.

Distance to the sun

890 million miles (1,433 million km) average.

Composition

Saturn is thought to have a core of iron and rock. Around this are layers of metallic hydrogen, liquid hydrogen, and helium.

Temperature

Temperatures at the top of Saturn's clouds average about -285°F (-175°C).

Surface gravity

About 0.93 times Earth's gravity.

Atmosphere

Saturn's atmosphere is about 93 percent hydrogen and 7 percent helium, plus traces of methane, ethane, ammonia, and various ices.

■ **Rhea is Saturn's second-biggest moon, and it seems to have a very faint, dusty ring, all of its own.**

Rhea is made of rock and water-ice, and is very cold. If you stood on the surface of Rhea, the ground under your feet would be a super chilly -281°F (-174°C).

■ GLOSSARY

Here are explanations for many of the terms used in this book.

Accretion The process by which stars and planets are thought to have formed. Dust particles bump into each other, stick together, and grow (accrete) into larger space objects. Planetesimals are the last stage of growth before becoming planets.

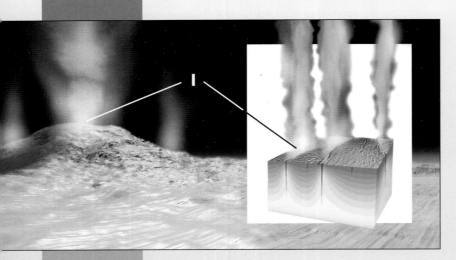

Atmosphere The layers of air surrounding most of the planets. Saturn's big moon Titan is the only moon with a thick atmosphere.

Aurora A glow in the sky caused by particles from the sun hitting a planet's magnetic field.

Comet A "dirty snowball" in space, made from a mixture of ice, dust, and rocks. The central part, or nucleus, may be smaller than a mile (1.6 km) across, to 30 miles (48 km) or more.

Core The center of a planet. The cores of Jupiter and Saturn are thought to be made mostly of iron, nickel, and rock.

Crust The hard, outermost layer of a rocky planet, such as Earth.

Frost line Space zone around the sun, between the orbits of Mars and Jupiter. Inside the line, water-ice vaporizes into a gas. Beyond the line, water-ice stays frozen.

Gas giant A large planet made mostly of gases, with no solid surface. Jupiter and Saturn are gas giants, along with the two outermost planets, Uranus and Neptune.

Geyser A plume of gas sprayed from under the ground.

■ **Astronomers who made early observations of Jupiter and Saturn included Galileo Galilei (1) and Giovanni Cassini (2), from Italy. Christiaan Huygens (3) came from Holland.**

Part of the sun to the same scale as the planets

1 2 3 4 5 6 7 8

Eddy Water, air, or smoke moving in a circle.

Gravity The universal force of attraction between all objects.

Halo a circle of light.

Helium The second most common element in the universe.

Hexagon A six-sided object.

Hydrogen The most common element in the universe. On the megaplanets, it is found as an atmospheric gas, as a liquid deep inside, and in metallic form around their cores.

Magnetic field The area of influence around anything that has magnetism.

Mass The amount of matter that an object contains.

Meteor A lump of rock drifting in space. If a big meteor hits a planet surface, it creates an impact crater.

Moon A space object that orbits a bigger one. Planets such as Jupiter and Saturn have many moons.

Orbit The curving path a space object takes around a more massive one, such as a planet orbiting the sun, or a moon moving around a planet.

Rocky planet A planet with a solid crust. Mercury, Venus, Earth, and Mars are all rocky planets.

Solar system The name for the sun and the eight major planets, dwarf planets, moons, and other space objects that circle it.

Volcano A mountain with a crater at its peak, through which gas and dust may spurt from under ground.

■ Here are the sun and major planets:
1 Mercury
2 Venus
3 Earth
4 Mars
5 Jupiter
6 Saturn
7 Uranus
8 Neptune

■ GOING FURTHER

Using the Internet is a great way to expand your knowledge of the megaplanets.

Your first visit should be to the site of the U.S. space agency, NASA. Its site shows almost everything to do with space, from the history of spaceflight to astronomy, and also plans for future missions.

There are also websites that give detailed space information. Try these sites to start with:

http://www.nasa.gov — The biggest space site.
http://saturn.jpl.nasa.gov — Cassini-Huygens.
http://www.space.com — Lots of stuff.
http://www.esa.int — European Space Agency.
http://www.spacedaily.com — Good for space news

■INDEX

Printed in the U.S.A.